Amazing Birds

by Molly Page

Table of Contents

Chapter I
Why Are Some Birds Amazing?

There are almost 10,000 different kinds of birds. Every bird has feathers and wings. Some birds are amazing because of what they can do, their size, or their colors.

⌒ This hummingbird is almost the same size as the flower.

Hummingbirds can do amazing things. They move their wings so quickly that these little birds seem to float in the air. Their beating wings make a humming sound.

Hummingbirds can fly in any direction—up, down, **forward**, and backwards. They have long beaks to help them get **nectar** from flowers.

🎧 Soon these baby ostriches will be as big as their parents!

Ostriches are amazing birds because of their size. They are the biggest birds in the world. They can grow to be nine feet tall.

An ostrich egg weighs about the same as two dozen chicken eggs.

Ostriches are also amazing because they do not fly like most birds do. They have long legs and are very fast runners. Female ostriches have the biggest eggs of all the birds.

The peacock's long feathers ⏎
are called a train.

Peacocks are amazing
birds because of their
colors. They have huge,
colorful **feathers** on
their backs. Peacocks
open and close their
feathers like a fan.
The colors seem to
sparkle when peacocks
fan their feathers.

Chapter 2

What Is Special About These Birds?

Roadrunners are very fast runners. They have very strong legs. They can be seen racing across roads. But, roadrunners soon move quickly out of the way of traffic. These birds can fly too, but mostly they run.

Roadrunners run to catch their food. They eat insects, small birds, snakes, mice, and lizards.

⬇ Roadrunners are about two feet long.

Owls are amazing birds because they sleep in the day. As soon as night falls, owls are awake. Owls look for food at night. Owls can't move their eyes to follow the animals they watch. They turn their heads.

⌒ Owls see and fly in the dark.

⬆ Owls use their sharp claws to hold onto their food.

Owls have good hearing, and they can hear when other animals are near. Owls do not make a sound when they fly. This helps them surprise any animal they hunt.

Eagles are amazing birds because of their **power**. They open their huge wings to fly. Eagles look very graceful when they fly.

Eagles eat other birds and small animals. They are very good hunters.

⬆ The bald eagle is the national bird of the United States of America.

⬆ The spread of an eagle's
wings can be up to eight feet wide.

Chapter 3

Why Are All Birds Amazing?

As you saw in this book, there are many different kinds of birds.

You saw huge, tiny, colorful, and very strong birds. In fact, every bird is amazing in its own way. So the next time you see a bird, think about why it is such an amazing animal.

Glossary

feathers *(FE-thuhrz)* the soft, light parts growing from a bird's skin *(page 6)*

forward *(FAWR-wuhrd)* in the direction ahead or in front *(page 3)*

nectar *(NEK-tuhr)* the sweet sugary liquid made by plants and used to make honey by bees *(page 3)*

power *(POW-uhr)* strength or force *(page 12)*

Index

Comprehension Check

Retell

Use a Make Inferences Chart to make an inference about birds.

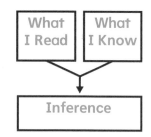

Think and Compare

1. Why can ostriches run so fast?

2. What birds have you seen? What is amazing about them?

3. Why do you think that scientists study different kinds of birds?